Praise fo

"A beautiful, mesmerizing collection. The supremely gifted Recinos is working the height of his formidable powers and *Cornered by the Dark* is a triumph."
—**Junot Díaz,** author of *The Brief Wondrous Life of Oscar Wao,* winner of the Pulitzer Prize and the National Book Critics Circle Award

"Recinos has always been a voice of compassion and orientation, a voice for dignity and justice. It is a voice that I have followed and admired over the decades. That voice reveals more depth and verve than ever in the present collection of poems. Indeed, 'cornered by the dark' as we all are in these times of social and cultural upheaval, these poems shed light, much light, much needed light, on a path forward."
—**Fernando F. Segovia,** Oberlin Graduate Professor of New Testament and Early Christianity, Vanderbilt University

"Archbishop Óscar Romero, lamenting government control of the media in El Salvador, preached from the pulpit that, 'A journalist either speaks the truth or he or she is no longer a journalist.' The same can be said of the poet. Harold Recinos, a worthy upholder of Romero's legacy, always speaks truth to power. In an age when the media self-censors for profit, and police departments continue to brutalize and execute black and brown bodies with impunity, Recinos draws deep from the wells of Latinx spirituality and urban experience to provide a vision of hope in the darkness—a vision in which the absence of God in the midst of human suffering is answered by the sacramentality of something as mundane as the Sunday movies."
—**The Rev. Dr. Rubén Rosario Rodríguez,**
professor of Theological Studies, Saint Louis University

"Harold Recinos' poems make visible the migrants and border-crossers, and the workers on whose labor we depend. He tackles all the tough subjects—loss, neighborhoods under threat, injustice and senseless violence, death. He also reminds us to search for what may endure—faith, family, and community. This book reminded me of all the reasons I love to read poetry and why I need to read more."
—**Maria Cristina Garcia,**
Professor of History and Latino Studies, Cornell University

Harold J. Recinos

CORNERED BY THE DARK

POEMS

IRON
PEN

PARACLETE PRESS
BREWSTER, MASSACHUSETTS

DEDICATED TO

Jose Gregorio Pineda Quinteros
and Emilia Reyes de Pineda
for their fierce witness to
our Crucified God

———————————

2021 First Printing

Cornered by the Dark: Poems

Copyright © 2021 by Harold J. Recinos

ISBN 978-1-64060-429-2

The Iron Pen name and logo are trademarks of Paraclete Press

Library of Congress Cataloging-in-Publication Data
Names: Recinos, Harold J. (Harold Joseph), 1955- author.
Title: Cornered by the dark : poems / Harold J. Recinos.
Description: Brewster, Massachusetts : Paraclete Press, 2021. | Series:
  Paraclete poetry | Summary: "Poetry capturing the marginal men, women,
  and children who tell their story about a culture of indifference, while
  finding courage and compassion to hope in everyday life"-- Provided by
  publisher.
Identifiers: LCCN 2021032224 | ISBN 9781640604292 | ISBN 9781640604308
  (mobi) | ISBN 9781640604315 (epub) | ISBN 9781640604322 (pdf)
Subjects: BISAC: POETRY / American / Hispanic & Latino | RELIGION /
  Christian Living / Social Issues | LCGFT: Poetry.
Classification: LCC PS3618.E4237 C67 2021 | DDC 811/.6--dc23
LC record available at https://lccn.loc.gov/2021032224

10 9 8 7 6 5 4 3 2 1

Published by Paraclete Press
Brewster, Massachusetts
www.paracletepress.com

Printed in the United States of America

CONTENTS

Home

I belong here
since the hour
my Puerto Rican
mother gave birth
and border-crossing
father fought Hitler
from floating U.S.
steel on the sea for
the grand old flag
he learned to pledge
like school kids in
the Bronx. I belong
to this land of first-
nation dreams, the
scars of those so
long enslaved, this
place the immigrants
come to live free, this
land on which my brother
died on a broken-English
street! I belong like the
dark hands that made
this country great, the
white faces fooled by
old men of greed, and
the deepest hope of
any dreamers' dream!
I belong, street lights
in the city said and the
first day here insists. I
belong like Lazarus
resurrected from the
dead.

Street Kid

it was past ten at Columbus Circle
when I realized night is filled with

memories not rescued by God for
the homeless. quietly, I embraced

everything about her in that time
of absence, saw her image in the

currents of wind blowing north on
Broadway and felt more deeply the

longing for home. I sat imagining
in the darkness mother would come

out of the subway station drowning
in tears for two lost boys, bells from

a church somewhere would begin to
ring and I would embark the awaited

journey to the apartment building in
the South Bronx to be once again with

the people who did not have English-
speaking tongues. I sat alone with the

night pretending to be a friend, not at all
understanding how each elapsed day

changes us. I sat until it ached on
that bench with my eyes stubbornly

on the subway exit telling myself
to simply hope! you probably will not

believe me but for more than fifty
years I missed this woman who

believed in Saints and still called
her mother.

The Parade

who said you live in the
barrio the day you showed

up on Fifth Avenue to see
the Saint Patrick's Day

Parade? was it the excluded
look in your eyes that gave

you away or how you turned
your head when somebody

yelled, *Yo spic!* did your
jacket with the Puerto Rican

flag on the back say it all
with its hint of the aroma of

green bananas you unloaded
from the truck parked in front

of the 110th Street bodega? I
bet it was the Spanglish cheers

you tossed to the brown-skinned
marchers of the fighting 69th that

today is browner than white and
Irish by adoption. faces laughing,

voices shouting, drums beating,
bagpipes playing, and there you

are saying every tribe in the city
is sucking in its breath like they

just showed up for a block party
in Spanish Harlem. I know you

walked over from Third Avenue
to watch, the street where little

kids already know how to gasp
a last breath, the barrio always

mocked by the city council that
does not believe the truth will

find people like you by the end
of the new century. Boricua,

I will cross the parade ground
and tell *los blanquitos* what you

told me one night on the stoop
with bugles blowing from an

old transistor radio in your left
hand that in the barrio you find

real light.

The Poor

you the poor from
everywhere an upright
God scattered on the
earth, who care for
children crying for
daily bread, scorned
by the bitter words
of the better-off who
never have known a
drink of such tears,
have the best view of
the humpbacked graying
men in governments
anywhere, thin on kindness
and distant from a divinity
that weeps. you dressed
with clothes coming apart
in threads, on all the walls
built to keep you out birds
will sweetly sing. there is
a place where the trembling
dissolves like a stream in
a rolling river that you will
recognize from all the photos
on your borrowed phone as
home.

The Visit

when I return to Home Street
on Easter Day after years that

have slipped into the wrinkles
on my face, will the things once

cherished still matter on the old
block? when I return from the

white world will you see me
like a ghost, reach out to touch

my brown face, search my pockets
for signs of life, tell me about the

children in the hands of death,
and those still alive? do you recall

sitting on the fire escape watching
people walking the sidewalk below

reciting the line from the Lord's
Prayer that says *on earth as it is in*

heaven, thinking that by saying it
with uplifted eyes the bent backs

on the block would straighten and
the cops would not tag a single kid

with brown skin a member of
the Turban Taps. when I return

on that day that was always so big
for the block, where the Spanglish

kids played on the sidewalk in new
ten-dollar clothes from Delancey

Street blaring as they ran *Jesus was
bilingual*, will you offer me a simple

piece of bread to feed the hunger no
other hand has touched? when I return

to visit let's have the stoop with
a little group of friends, junkies,

and girls from the families that
died penniless take part in it so we

can talk about whatever is left
to dream.

Shots

across the border where
the dead were left on a
Walmart floor by a young
white man full of hate and
ageless sin, we breathed the
poison air and shed tears of
ancient grief. on the earth of
a Texas border town beneath
the grass cut by Latinx hands
for more years than English ever
noises made, cold white fingers
answered the Devil's roll call by
murdering innocent dark-skinned
shoppers with Spanish-sounding
names. as you bow your heads
to pray holding other warm hands
keep in mind the crawling worms
and rotting death that welcomed
our beloved to the foulest dusty
bed. when you kneel at the altar
remember the sound of weeping
and the punctured faith of those
who survived the fired shots.

I Woke

like the first day at
Orchard Beach with
music played to fill
us with magnificent
feelings of belonging.
that first walk to the
Valencia Bakery to
get yesterday's bread
for free to eat with a
twenty-five cent butter
stick with Nuyorican lips
that trembled with life. the
walk to the public school
for a first-time pledge for
teachers seeing only the
outside of us. and that
bright day on the stoop
we realized America is
home. Lord, we are glad
for this moon, sun, air,
earth and piece of long
forgotten stoop.

Snow

snowfall came slowly
overnight, soundless.

you could see the flakes
bit by bit floating down

blanketing the street white.
I stood watching the cloud

work from the window that
made the avenue heavier by

the hour. the morning lights
fell softly on the heads of

the Puerto Rican children,
playing. for a brief moment,

I experienced the goodness of
the world and time worth selling

to a forgetful God. I knew the
day would not go on with its

business, the apartments would
be singing and the sayings of the

wise would get freshly painted
on the telephone building wall,

again. I saw from the window
truth was on the street tossed like

a ball to deliver a blessing to
the poor bones on our sweet,

sweet block.

Speechless

yes,
I am afraid to
see more fleeing
faces banished
from the English-
speaking world,
a southern border
turned into hate,
the pale faces of
nationalists, moons
that come and go
without delivering
a flicker of hope.
yes,
I am afraid to
see covers for so
much light, brown
bodies on the roads
never leading to
paradise, the voices
buried in cells that
are not allowed to
speak, the governors
that rule with cruelty
and
lies and sorrow
sucking
dry the beautiful poor's
dreams.

yes,
I am afraid of all the
blindness, the distant
freedom, the shameless
equality, and the walls
with razors and nails
sparkling in the sun
like America unable
truthfully to speak!

The Blind Man

the blind old man whose
eyes are touched nightly

by stars walks himself to
Simpson Street every day

at first sun. he taps here
and there on the sidewalk,

listens to the South Bronx
world rushing around him

and hears everything more
clearly than others ever take

the time to get. he does not
lose his way! he walked that

morning with faith around his
wrinkled neck without a touch

of doubt, a cross hanging from
a thin gold chain, worn to keep

watch for oracular surprises that
suddenly rise as they often do

on the street. he kept time each
morning listening to a distant

Cathedral striking its bells and
heard on the walks more Spanish

confessions than any of the local
priests, it seemed. the blind man

the people on the block thought
was a petition for their darkest

hours reminding everyone each
day with a sacramental humility

to just live.

Lost

this street,
how familiar it is to me.
the corner tenement has
become a shooting gallery
with agents of dope in the
apartments where just a
few years ago mothers
put flower vases on the
fire escapes and raised
kids. this street was
populated for years
with household gods that
trembled into the morning
hours. it has become the
latest Spanglish town where
people vanish into the
shadows. this street the
Most High God has not
descended from heaven to
see. this street, adorned
by unending light from
the night sky has known
children at play, mothers left
weeping and itself like a lost
child in a wooded park. this
street has for too long bent
with forfeited Brown lives.

Tisha B'Av

in the voices of children
playing in the schoolyard,
the blowing wind carrying
mothers' tears to wash the
world clean, the images of
clouds pushed over borders
for longer than anyone will
live, we crave with migrants—
the weary, the sick and the
weak—the kindness that says
we are all human beings. in
the words spoken in darkness,
each prayer breathed into the
stale prison air, the finality of
the innocent who rest in graves,
the unending hush of the great
American Cathedrals, we admit
the lavish tables with plenty to
eat are not well-tutored in the
story of the God who invites the
wretched to a great feast. in the
silent screams familiar to the Jew
on a cross, the crooked old men
drawing all the light in the nation
into their ashy skin, we will walk
with you through hell to the river
carving a course to a new Eden.

Words

what more can I say about
the fool who lived in a 5th
Avenue tower, the clowns
who parade around him in
the name of a white-cleansed
history and the world that
cries with the eyes of migrant
children? what more can I say
of the twisted voices racially
dividing, the weak who suffer
State villainy and the pounding
hearts of mothers who scream
for dead children? what can I tell
you about the boy holding a toddler's
picture in front of him in a day-
long funeral march, the strings that
play in the pit and the satisfied
old men with power who look
away content? when will you
chant for us *there is a balm in
Gilead* and chariots will lead us
sweetly home?

The Box

she left her heart behind
in the church in case God

happened by one day to
visit the harsh dark space

to find it. it would exist
for her remotely beating

behind the figure of the
sacred Mother with her

sweet name. when taken
out of the tiny black box

where she laid it the good
Lord would be struck by the

way love in it never ends.
when she got to the land

with a different sky at the
end of her long walk her

heart started beating once
for each line of sorrow seen

on her face. she learned to
ride the subways mumbling

to herself something about
blistered feet recalling time

traveled with ghostly images
in every step that insisted on

telling their names. she lived
in a room with nine other girls

in her full dark skin, working
by day and crying in the lonely

night about El Norte where a
life like hers was tossed like

unwanted pennies. yet, every
night just before drifting into

sleep the faces of her children
came into view and she could hear

the distant beating of her heart
alive and well in the village church

and her two boys calling out
for her from their deep brown

dreams that carefully explained
everything beneath her Spanish-

speaking sky.

El Norte

the caravan departs today
for the near uncrossable

border, the smell of sweet
fruit juices in the air on a

dim village street, chattering
mothers with infant in arms

debating what is right, youth
preparing to emerge from the

years of being buried beneath
English lies, and a local priest

on hand with a prayer to blow
the walkers clear of the words

from harsh white tongues. the
migrants in the greatest homeless

history ever told, the inheritors of
the earth who suffer poverty, endure

rape, experience hunger, grieve
death, flee violence, and are the

world's slaves with unwanted dark
skin rush to the border to find a

place further than had ever been
imagined from home. they are on

the move with blistered feet toward the
North country that committed crimes

for more than a century on their Spanish-
speaking streets while singing of liberty,

equality and freedom with deftly tied
strings and not a single lick of shame.

Julia

her name was Julia and
on Friday she painted her
nails to end the burden of
a long week of hard work
downtown. she sat for
hours on the stoop telling
stories that recalled voices
slowly disappearing in
the spaces that separated her
from the hamlet where the
many poor still live beneath
the unsung glory of a vague
heaven. she was made to scatter
private tales in the South Bronx,
to share Spanish mysteries never
heard before on a street named
to honor the man who wrote, more
than a century ago, *The Song of
Hiawatha*. the frightened street
received her tales that magically
pasted themselves to the wall on
Tito's building beside the mural
coated last year for the Day of the
Dead. the innocent days of children
on the block were drawn to her like
the moon tide that rushed to shore
while stars shivered. I looked for her
in the immense silence that remained
the day she disappeared. I yelled her
name into all of the places where on
this block something was lost.

The Kid

I went up the station
stairs at 2 a.m. chilled
by winter.

I swore the train lights
were running north on
the steel tracks.

I boarded the unheated
train where a girl with
a torn bag sat.

I heard silence broken by
the constant clanging of
wheels.

I was glad in the city of hard
labor for brown hands not
to be alone.

The Café

the air outside was stark cold
and people filled the Café with

answers. Olga sat on a corner
stool at the end of the bar, the

salsa was already playing, the
timbalero who never missed a

well-placed beat had ecstasy
coming out of his eyes, yellow

horns played beautifully enough
to make the Puerto Ricans in the

room drop their heavy loads and
white faces nearly turned the color

of earth. in the lyrical atmosphere
of the space with the best lower

east side musicians on stage I could
see this would be a good place to

begin a history book of the salsa
age. in the middle of the room,

with rhythms falling from the high
ceiling, dancers magically circled

the floor with delicious widened
feelings that rendered their brown

souls naked. the voices in the room
with sweet accents had no need for

crass English good housekeeping
seals, these people of mine who come

from a long line of slaves that broke
chains are in the room taking their time

dreaming up light.

Thanksgiving Day

on this day of sitting around
tables to give thanks to the

earth for gifts I had a vision
of the people who loathe the

Spanish-speaking poor, I heard
the violated earth coughing for

fresh air, rich old men stuffing
their mouths with capital gains,

the justice of this land's ancient
ways pushed deeper into idolaters'

freshly dug graves, the blood of
first nation's ancestors flowing

in rivers, white ropes dangling
black and brown bodies from

big trees, and pale faces believing
their nation will not be judged by

the Crucified Lord who sits on a
heavenly throne. on a day like this

an Angel will come blowing a
trumpet to wake the quick and the

dead and the liars in high places
across the land will stain their pants

in fear of God's coming fire. soon,
we will hear the trampled beneath

expensive shoes cry out *impenitent*
sinners who keep yourselves beyond

the reach of the Lord's love impatiently
hell waits for you. on this day of

sitting around tables we give thanks
for prayers, the things kindly given

in alms, the Great Spirit with open
hands, and the crying in us that

knows who listens.

The Big Clock

when the big clock on the Banco
de Ponce stopped last year gossip

circled the streets that it was a sign.
the street hustlers used it to discuss

theories of time choking in the South
Bronx. the neighborhood philosopher

insisted it was a mirror of the clock
on our backs dividing us from the rest

of the city. the swearing kids on the
block never noticed it relying on the

simplicity of night and day to measure
their experience of things. no one ever

referred to the broken timer to explain
where they had been, what they should

have said yesterday and how the future
was quite near. that big clock never

held our dreams, could never learn to
count in Spanish or chime a fine day

for the block. when we listened for the
hours the chanting moon and whispers

in the wind loudly ticked their truths
and that was enough for us to keep

searching for the promises made at
the beginning when God did not

weep.

Street Name

on Loisaida Avenue the
Caribbean island survivors

emerged from the ashes of
their nameless dead with

vivid memories of relatives,
friends, teachers and priests

living in their hearts, born to
a world of madness, rejection,

seasonal joys, stumbling with
old junkies on the way to the

roof for a high, visiting funeral
homes close to the block with

awful tears for the latest kid
stripped of life in a country

of thinning freedom. we used to
call the street Avenue C until

Spanglish tongues took over, and
heaven threatened anyone who

denied a Puerto Rican presence on
lower Manhattan streets. the congas

now play in the park, cleansing whatever
tries to break these poor hearts, the sweet

drumming in the neighborhood declaring
Puerto Ricans will endure long past the

day history is last written about
Nueva York.

Advent

every night the wind blows
the winter a little closer to

us, and I begin to think of
the little drummer boy, the

lines of scripture about Mary
and Joseph with an infant in

arms fleeing to Egypt, the
precious story of an Angel

who spoke in a dream of Herod's
treachery aiming to take innocent

lives, and the talk out of the great
silence of the coming time of peace

with a justice worldly despair
could not withstand. I think of

the baby in a manger unable yet
to utter words, vulnerable like

the radically hospitable God that
does not leave us, and the gracious

star that still leads us toward more
hopeful ground in the name of truth

too lofty for words. there is a presence
on these chilly nights, a Spirit moving

with the certainty that was even before
time, and I hear news whispered that

life is beaded with grace.

The Ruins

I strolled into the ancient field,
the site archeologist was smiling

from a dig, school children ran
alongside the sloping walls of the

Mayan ball court with Itzamná's
creation beneath their feet, they

stopped often to look at the sky
with the same birds in flight that

appeared to them in nightly dreams,
and in wooded places marked by the

traces of those who once lived in
that place. I climbed an ancient

pyramid to look across the great
valley catching a glimpse of the

land beyond where my ancestors
I am told wait. there I conjured stories

till night came along, leaned into a
wind carrying the sweet low-pitched

chatting of animals roaming the
surrounding Mayan forest, listened

to the calm singing of black-eyed
leaf frogs and learned a bit more

about how to remove thorns in
my side to better walk on the

babbling sidewalks of cities with
shouting white lips fiercely

saying *Get out!*

Panic

there is a note of panic in
your voice about the Holy

Land you walked away from
in Central America because

God could not figure out how
to stop the day's threatening to

become another anxious farewell
story. I can hear your beating

heart made from deep down
thoughts looking for signs of

peace, no longer whispering
the words tasting of ashes in

your mouth, insisting with
firm faith a decent new life is

about to begin. what words
can I summon to mend your

incomplete years, to overthrow
mounting woes, and assure you

sweet heaven will stir for you
on this brown earth? each minute

detonates with screams coughed
from memories of the night you

slipped away from a kind home,
and now I can only promise to

wait for the wind to whisper to
me words that will caress your

scorched heart.

Sagrada Familia

on Second Avenue a mother,
father and boy stroll slowly

down the sidewalk like the
world is watching them to

the steps at the abandoned
church where the police just

yesterday chased them away.
when grace descends to the

empty building, pedestrians
may place coins in the old

hat the man placed in front
of them and they will feel a

familiar happiness like the
sky lit up with stars in the

evening back in their tiny
Spanish-speaking village.

this Holy family makes you
wonder who holds the celestial

blueprint that tells us something
better is coming, when wintry

night will disclose her unspeakable
secrets to their broken English

dreams, how long they will need
to brace themselves in the land

that wishes to see them entirely
undone? the moon watches over

the Pineda family tonight, far off
seasonal carolers stumble through

O Come All Ye Faithful, while the
people walking past the family on

the condemned building steps
have a vague impression in their

eyes that all the mute mysteries
on aloof church shelves are about

to lavishly speak.

Numeritos

we glide on the subway
tracks steadily moving
uptown toward the place
called home with thoughts
threading together a past
world. we surface from
Manhattan's tunnel to see
the projects withdraw as
the train pulls into the next
bleached wood station, a man
tosses in his seat talking to
himself to crush feelings of
loneliness and we look around
to see who prays for god to
fold into the rail car. curving
the tracks in the distance the
church steeple is visible enough
to our cracked eyes to make us
ask about the dead carpenter who
never worked and the gods made
downtown with money. before
reaching the exit station, we talk
about last night's dreams, the visits
in them from the dead, and the
numbers they shared for a lottery
ticket to beat the odds.

The Walk

we could spend the time
walking First Avenue to

China Town talking on
the edges of unfamiliar

blocks and letting the
words fall from our tongues

to bounce like a Spaulding
handball on the old city

sidewalk. we could pause
in front of the synagogue

nestled on the bottom floor
of Tito's apartment building

looking like a Pentecostal
storefront that is attended

by the owner of Moishe's
pastry shop to ask for a

divine sign. maybe you
would prefer to walk hand

in hand without saying a
single word, smiling at the

birds spying us from their
fire escape perches, with

eyes open to people trying
to love themselves. the truth

it doesn't matter what street
we take so long as the light

keeps playing with you and
I can share a thousand stories

with a simple look.

A Barrio New Year

after fifty-two long weeks
we have reached the end of

the year when you forget the
long list of regrets, look into

a new beginning and wish others
the best and all that crap. we

will be fixed on the ball that
drops at Times Square from

what used to be called the Allied
Chemical Building when the

world seemed more innocent, ok
Shorty lived on 167th Street

shooting dope, and the area
cop who walked the beat was

called by bodega Joe, Flatfoot.
you know Milagro waited two

full years for the Pentecostal
coyote to bring across three

borders her two young boys
who will celebrate their first

Feliz Año Nuevo on the cold
block. tonight, she will carry

flowers in the darkness to the
church just before a new time

is birthed, utter simple prayers
for promises fulfilled, and tell

the Supreme Sufferer they will
embrace new hopes and the life

they cannot yet see. we long
for truth to be gathered into

a great big ball and dropped
downtown as snow falls from

a cloudy sky for the world to raise
a glass of manifold peace and

cheer!

Ismael

night itself could not
find sleep with all the

sounds in Spanish that
echoed in the hallway

causing a few pious souls
to jump from beds in prayer.

eyelids refused to be sealed
by the hand of heaven while

voices in the stairwell shouted
in the name of a bully God. the

gossipers were hollering about
Margarita's son like tomorrow

was too anxious to hear. the show
lasted more than an hour making

the apartment dwellers think the
worst things of the boy who had

come out. we walked to school
most days, worked the garment

district summers, and lit candles
on his mother's bedroom altar

which made the lady smile. the
fools screaming in the hallway

were too stupid to admit Ismael
was made by God like anybody

in the world. bless you Ismael
for telling the stone throwers

on the church steps your way of
loving does not lessen a thing.

The Pastor

they arrived rejoicing up
the hill to listen to a pastor
churn up stories of truth like
the earth they worked. the light
in the sanctuary appeared real
thick in the room where words
breathed the sweetest news of
things to believe. the pastor
spoke into the shadows while
people thought of wandering
in good faith. they arrived in
that cloudy church to hear the
pastor full of care deliver patient
mid-morning prayers that moved
them to places worth their secret
longing. they left after more than
an hour taking shortcuts to places
called home.

Sunday Clothes

every Sunday the good clothes
kept in the bottom drawer and

on the same wooden hanger in
the closet came out. the button

on the white shirt worn by the
boy to Mass was still missing

though no one in the local house
of worship noticed. they all

went to the Cathedral eager each
week to wake in the dim excitement

of yet another service full of big
promises with deep responses to

the mystery that called so many
to make heavenly requests. the

minutes in the basement of the
place of worship scurried past the

well-dressed boy with little new
knowledge given and the bell's

last call that rang in his small ears
unable to explain why his father

was still in jail. for the little boy
in his Sunday best the pulpit held

no secrets and the words spoken from
it bounced off the Stations of the Cross

decorating the walls. the little boy
kept waking himself up just to make

sure he was actually in church and not
in his crowded bed still sleeping. his

mother finally went to the altar
to light candles for Holy Mary and

the child thought no power in heaven
will keep him from outgrowing his

fancy threads.

Holy Mother

the flight came so suddenly
though the gangs and Herod's

thugs who roamed the village
streets of the darkened country

trampled about with sinfulness.
she trembled with an infant in arms

thinking of the long march north
and rumors that unpacked bibles

will not prevent the border cops
from prying her fingers from a

child. the days of keeping silent
and begging to hear the soft voice

of the Mother of God delivering
a message of salvation retreat with

each single step. she will arrive
with stories of the violence in all

her days, the history of American
war crimes against the helpless of

a nation that did not lift for them
the light. she will not understand

imprisonment, her infant's name not
spoken, the number designations to

be given, the new face of fear in
jail and the mockery of the English-

speaking nation for the rescuing
blood of Christ. each night she

will kneel down in a cell with tears
for her child, pleading for heaven's

chariot to come quickly to steal her
and the innocent who cry away.

Sunday Movies

they walked sweetly talking
of their endless river of dreams

while snowflakes dropped from
the sky. when they reached the

corner a woman exited a bodega
to empty a bucket of water and

brightened their faces with her
smile. the pace got slower when

they saw Manolo just home from
the Viet Nam war between two

parked cars taking a leak and arguing
with the snow blanketing the same

hat that just last night was run over
by the Westchester Avenue bus. they

talked music, the Puerto Rican girls,
el cuchifrito restaurant dishing out

sofrito hope, little kids turning into
junkie men, Joey who came out of

jail with a Muslim name and America
still at war. the buildings listening

behind them trembled uncontrollably
each time questions bounced off their

old cracked walls. they arrived at the
box office of the Star Movie House,

where the hollow tree was planted
and held carved names on its side,

gave the old Jewish ticket lady a
bunch of change and made their way

to the auditorium to make the three
shows playing a part of their lives for

one Sunday afternoon. they
sat quietly in the fourth row

of seats gathering into themselves
new stories like they were pearls

in the sand of Orchard Beach.

Due North

in the hallway you can hear
the muffled barking of a dog
coming from the third floor,
the halting footsteps of new
migrants to these New York
Spanglish streets, and the tiny
sacred brown feet of clay that
belong to the shouting children.
they stared down the dark days
ahead last week by the border
fence, turned their faces north
and followed the shivering birds
across the border in search of
a quiet spot to reminisce about their
longed-for home. the miraculous
warming sun and silver-freckled
dark sky will welcome them young
and old without papers, the puppet
officials in high office will want to
toss them bitter bread, and before
the nation is drained of color the
defenders of the weak will give
voice to their tales.

Epiphany

I quickly took a seat on the
stoop staring at the clock on

the Dollar Savings Bank just
to catch one glimpse of time

on the run. I settled for split
seconds full of purpose that

left me more white-haired on
Southern Boulevard in that

Spring morning. I sat on the tilted
steps with a copy of *The Hobbit*

given to me by a white kid in
California and looked up

the street expecting Puerto Rican
dwarfs to come walking along

singing about bent forks and
cracked plates just to mock

the city. I sat quietly and saw
light trickle down the face of a

widow gently leading her steps
to the social services building at

the end of the block and then felt
troubled not to know her sweet

name. she left a fragrance in the
air surrounding me, the scent of

migrant dreams and the aging face
of freedom replete with unbearably

complete answers.

The Flight

the pigeons flew overhead
half asleep in a large flock

on the way to the leaky roof
at the elevated subway station.

their hardly stretched wings
made the distance while the

blessed wind rounding the
Simpson Street corner sang

news that had nothing to do
with Spanish dreams. before I

knew it my thickening eyes
conceived the summer clouds

with rain, despised brown-skinned
kids standing at the start of their

lives, the rising stars saying not
a word about God and the vain

searching taking place in the fine
old church, where water was once

poured on our heads. twisted truth
on these streets, old gods that hardly

existed for us, glorious mysteries down
here unreasonably told. when will you

free us from the dark prescriptions
of America? Sweet Lord, can you

yet deliver us from the malefactors
and despisers mutilating us with pale-

faced lies?

The Hidden Face

the past speaks in a thin
voice against forgetting

calling out pictured names
that are often standing in

place, quietly arranging the
way you see the new world

that says you were never
meant to be human. you

spend each day worried
about the stranger things of

politics like accented speech,
the color of your skin, the

length of the footsteps that
got you here and just how

close this country really is
to this God who stays far

away from your deepest
prayers. you used to enter

churches to speak freely,
discover kind messages to

mend your wounded soul,
listen to music that helped

ripen dreams, but now errors
meet you when you visit the

English halls of worship that
erase you with unforgiving

stares. I saw you kneeling at
the altar with others and you

whispered a prayer about being
made in the likeness of a dark

God who crawled down your
mutilated streets and detests

white thrones.

Language Lesson

Spanglish is the language
of these streets for the new

generation that can see the
lights downtown from the

rooftops and their place in
America ordained by the

steadfast stars. on the gray
sidewalks you hear the code-

switch shouts wailing against
the English-only tongues that

forget to think. the brown flesh
lobs words into the open from

its lips to decompose the white
tyranny imposing darkness on

the inner city kids. la bodega
hoards two languages like the

church bells that ring in the new
day, splitting the knots picked

up at school, and sprinkling these
tongues with the scented barrio

memories that never shed tears.
frankly, you cannot mock this new

speech that wraps the sweetly
hyphenated patois born with the

Latinx young. one hundred years
from now the churches will sing

the best hymns in Spanglish, the
University will teach rhetoric in

a bilingual tongue and presidents
will mix it up like they do at the

Perez bodega to talk about the
asombroso smorgasbord called

the American dream.

Street Fair

I remember the crowded street
in Little Italy with the procession

marchers chanting prayers quite
low while others watched, telling

tales. on this New York City street
the prayers are not the same to the

wood carved Saint like they were in
the beginning, though the sighs from

the ancient desert are still audible on
the corners. I walked the open air

festival in honor of Saint Anthony
to China Town, the church doors

were open for pedestrians to enter,
the other Saints scattered about the

sanctuary reminding me they left the
world with enough sins to keep it

worried. I kept looking for the great
light to shine around the image of

Saint Anthony carried by the pious
with dollars fit beneath a bunch of

rubber bands affixed to him, wondered
who in the crowded fair ever felt lost,

begged forgiveness or gave a thought
to God. then, I felt the breeze on its

way uptown saying, *be still, the light*
darkening in the world will overwhelm

things with questions and lead flesh
home.

Gethsemane

tonight, music plays in
the lower East Side café
and the trombone forgets
silence.

people crowd the bar's counter
with a picture of my old friend
in a cheap frame against a dim
mirror.

the 3rd Street door opens to
add visitors to the room and
wind blows in me to your place
of absence.

then, the diasporic salsa band
calls us to push back the rickety
chairs to sway and moan on
weary feet.

tonight, bitterness fades like
the scraped knee on a playful
child and the tenements on the
block have no names.

I like this café where night is
never the same, lovers explain
music and poets light the room
with words.

God

the little boy spent the day
alone in the apartment with

the front door without a key
talking to God who had a

soft voice with a Spanish
accent and was closer to him

than the religious altar where
he sometimes knelt. he never

got a look at the divine face
though that did not keep him

from rapping away like the
heavenly figure was sitting

on the stoop watching the
bus rush down Westchester

Avenue. the little boy asked
the accented voice with him

in the locked apartment, is it
true there are no secrets in life,

that big pitted stones can speak,
people like little Tito who turned

to dust will one day soon return
and the dusty faces on the block

will find reasons to pass out
bits of their homemade dreams

like flan? God the great help to
ages past leaned over and oddly

did not speak—the boy thought
God just forgot how to live

among the poor.

Unthinkable

On Sunday walking to
church holding hands

weighing little, a mother
looked at her boys and

wept. even then she was
fleeing those who rush

to hate, the fear handed
to her each day, the prison

that waited for her crying
and the liberty that took flight

with wings. after so many
years in church she still did

not understand why the good
Lord preferred to hear words

manufactured by her wounded
heart than to see it whole. the big

Cathedral sermons leave her in
the dark, the conquered faces in

the Spanish Mass held in the
basement of the Hoe Avenue

Church projecting more bad
news. she wept, insisting with

each tear that, if God does exist, then
the lunacy on this earth she has

to walk daily should draw that
presence near. I saw her last week

and she is still waiting for good
news to find her overcrowded

room, rotted floors, hungry kids
and ICE knocking on the door.

La Plaza

while we
waited in
the town square
the park
workers
found
the best
shade by
a leafy tree
to cool themselves
from
municipal employment.
they laughed
to comfort
their
weary hands
the patch
of
flowers
they planted
that very
morning
wide-spread
in the
Mesoamerican
sun.
our eyes
fell on the
cathedral's
cupola slanting
to the left

and a Bible-
holding preacher
wheedling
a small crowd
to believe
in his
distant
U.S.-made
monolingual
God.

Rubble

there was a building here
once where these cracked
bricks, splintered wood,
rusty nails and wrecked
toys lay. the artifacts of
future archeology for the
spics who were daily cast
away from a world that
said their lives are of no
importance. the winter
frost is preserving the
rubble that in the South
Bronx has seen many years
of dark. the celestial gods
have overlooked it, the lily
white people downtown not
seen it, and neighboring love
never bothered with its world
of bruises and loss.

Created

in the morning the foreign
tongues in this tenement

begin. each has a story of
another life full of savage

disharmonies that crash on
English-only ears. yesterday

the old Jewish man on the
first floor shouted out to me

shalom then offered it means
peace. I smiled at him on the

way to pick up spices at the
bodega and saw him wipe his

cheek of tears. in the morning
the first floor of the block church

is filled by God's sightseers who
only speak English and whisper

disbelief that divinity blew to life
more worlds than they with all

their piety dare see. in the
morning when God wakes up

earlier than words the world
missed must look so very, very

different.

Apathy

I looked up at the stars
one early morning on the

streets downtown expiring
by the hour in the valley of

skyscrapers without a place
in a rich country to call home.

the vain language in the big
church on Fifth Avenue painted

pictures street kids like me living
with uncertainty in the dark ever

believed spoke anything but dumb
crap. the buildings on Broadway

were all lit up as if in an imperialist
parade, the brokers delighted by the

numbers rising and the noise of the
poor just an unimportant audience to

dismiss. I looked up at the dotted sky
with fading night that appeared to me

like a million watchful eyes blessed
my worn-out shoes and filthy clothes

and told the church in the land east of
Eden still ringing its bells in my teenage

head the poor inherit nothing.

Slain on the Altar

how long in this feverish time
will ignorance give flight to

knowledge too fearful to speak
about the shameful triumph of

idols that beat the humanity out
of the weak? will the old river

waters carry away the stinging
in ailing hearts on the run to

allow them hushed peace on
the other side? how many weeks

must pass before the bandages
on injured souls are removed

and a new year swings open to
make them delirious with liberty

and life? when will the shackles
dragged around each day in this

place yield the thorny lanes to
a precious emancipated state that

demolishes the walls hate builds
with the quiet dignity of truth?

when will the mocking uniformed
men, sadistic office-bearers and

citizens excited to punish learn to
stop sucking blood from the poor

and give the brown children of God
a welcome? well, some say beneath

a field of stars in this hymn-singing
America the dark and wretched

time will never end.

Genesis

the world is divided
into countries.

the people are separated
by languages.

the children are parted
by their names.

the multicolor ancestors
loiter in the dark.

the noise is heard inside
crushed dreams.

the ghost-ridden lanes
for the dark skinned.

the border a place for
the gas canisters.

the swastika faces like
stones thrown.

the land unlawful
swelling into view.

the fragrant earth
falling into silence.

Translated Signs

you may not mind the
words in the Bible that

after all are sounds put
in place by translated

signs. the long passages
you've likely heard at

the oddest times still
hanging on the back

of your tongue may even
cough up regular images

from time to time with
expectations admittedly

wrenched from another
world. you may recount

history with it, stumble
empires with its lens and

flay the morality of the
sinister politicians with

its pages. the sounds so
simply made by those

ancient words that make
many marvels perhaps you

agree can still move heavy
stones, disclose wonder and

send us off with imagination
and a sweeter taste of life

on our lips to walk the dusty
streets.

Lament

who
now
can say
the
dwelling
place of
God
on earth
opens
its arms
like a
sweet
sparrow's
wings?
who
today
can
believe
the tatty
church
bells
are
heard
beyond
the
pale-faced
moon?
who
now
can say

they
know
the
names
of
those
with
loving
hearts
slain
in
the name
of
a God
that
doesn't
soak us
all
with
Grace?
who
now
can say
in
the
evening
hours
Christ
does not
weep

with
outcasts
in all
the
places
of
sweet
forbidden
love?

Broken

I lift one leg after another
to make it down the street

past an Alleluia storefront
with no desire to enter the

holy room before reaching the
corner the abuelitas on the block

call Calvary. I heard them in the
storefront one night read *The Lord*

is my Salvation though the rescue
didn't last beyond your fourteen

years, so we painted your name on
a wall and prayed God could read.

you never made it out of childhood,
escaped the deadly spring nor listened

too long to the insulting words of the
pedantic scholars of the city streets

that now your premature death to a
different world indicts. let me stand

here a little longer with you my dear
brown child of God. receive these tears

dropping from my face to flood the
world with your nightmare. I promise

you and the swooping angels who
know this corner well to talk about

the days you lived, this dastardly time
that saddens us and who knows maybe

a lost and found resurrection.

Beloved

rest
your
crying
soul
on me,
the
beauty
with care
too deep,
fools said,
for
God.
lay
your
injured
heart
on my
shoulder
while
those who
know
too
little of
love pass
to the
world
of God's
surprises.
whisper
to me

now
you
know God
pressed
you into
life.

The Hidden Face

the past speaks in a thin
voice against forgetting

calling out pictured names
that are often standing in

place quietly arranging the
way you see the new world

that says you were never
meant to be human. you

spend each day worried
about the stranger things of

politics like accented speech,
the color of your skin, the

length of the footsteps that
got you here and just how

close this country really is
to this God who stays far

away from your sincere
prayers. you used to enter

churches to freely speak,
discover kind messages to

mend your wounded soul,
listen to music that helped

ripen dreams, but now errors
meet you when you visit the

English halls of worship that
erase you with unforgiving

stares. I saw you kneeling at
the altar with others whispering

a prayer about being made in the
likeness of this brown earth.

Freeman Street

it was a long walk back
from West Farms Road

to the new apartment on
the boulevard. the kids in

front of Valencia Bakery
with drooling appetites on

their pale lips shared a piece
of yesterday's bread in front

of John F. Kennedy's picture
displayed on the bread shop's

window. we walked with a
huge bundle of silence, worried

about wearing out the soles on
our shoes, telling stories heard

at the Ponce Social Club from old
men who wept reading the morning

news, and imagining Nelson who
fled the South Bronx rubble at the

Job Corps Center in Texas finding
the pieces for a better life. we

passed the Freeman Street subway
Station, recalling out loud days spent

at the Boys Club beside it, the cop
with the wrinkled shirt who walked

you home the night the city blacked
out and the Pentecostal worshipers

shouting the end of the world. we kept
walking down the Southern Boulevard,

nodding our heads when we passed
the elementary school that had not yet

helped the history of our streets, while
trying to gather up what remained of

daylight to stuff into our pockets. we
got to the building on Mapes Avenue

questioning for a long time what comes
next.

Worship

on Sunday there is
a lot of singing in the
church where finely dressed
people gather to confess God
only knows what. little kids
sit in the last pew whispering
in Spanish and giggling at the
old women who love to throw
their arms in the air with open
hands like they are playing
catch with the Holy Spirit. by
the time the choir begins to sing
little Tito has sketched his idea
of the preacher who spent more
than thirty minutes sweating up
words to approach the distant
mystery mothers dragged us out
to see. we are surrounded by
repentant adult sinners who leave
the sanctuary with looks on their
faces like children who just shared
a big old secret.

The Distance

the bright sun rested its
head in the village shade
feeling a cool wind blow
past its burning face long
enough to listen to the old
man, in the fourth house of
a back street, talking about his
only daughter who marched
to the Capital of the United
States, untutored in big city
life and the high-priced admission
demanded by a country that still
thinks its illness along with the
buried pieces of the Mesoamerican
dead will not be noticed. I have
sat in that house noticing even
on the brightest days the sky is
dark, the earth seems to tremble
and the wind rustling the leaves
of two trees beside what the old
man calls a porch saying in their
mysterious way from where they
stand—we miss her! I have sat
with this old man who suffers
death without expiring reading
bible verses, threatening God with
disbelief and begging for the sake
of this daughter living far away in
North country to be fed honey from
rocks.

Save

for the children who
died in the detention
camps who no longer
dream, save a place at
your table. for strangers
who took their lives in
American-made cells, save
a place at your table. for
the people you only think
of once a week in prayer,
save a place at your table.
for the mothers who come
from villages without names,
save a place inside of you.
for the poor from the cities
never reached by pitying
voices, save a place in your
books. for the people no one
knows who live, let them cross
the border.

The Bells

I can hear the sound of
church bells ringing in
the perfect day you made
with all that matters in it.
they reach across the vast
city spaces clanging pious
chimes of a different world
near reach. I hear the people
talking Spanish dressed in old
clothes walking the sidewalks
until descending night welcoming
your clear peace. I can see a black-
dressed widow walking past the
dream-selling bodegas with a rosary
in a dark wrinkled hand muttering
all the joys in her life and pausing on
stoops to caress the children on the
block with your perfectly indulging
love.

Holding Hands

at night the windows fell
dark with sleep, the level

of dreams took their place
on the wretched bench at

the corner of the park the
tattooed white girls never

walked at night, the hapless
odors from rubbish cans

floated uptown and alone
my thirteen years abruptly

sent away, hollered. I lay
awake nights in my filthy

rags to weep, remembering
the crowded rented space

with an altar full of ceramic
Saints, two siblings who danced

in mirrors, and a single mother
living revised psalms of lament

far too young to be penitent. I
walked the park today so many

years later with my daughter
holding my hand. we laughed,

talked and noticed how beauty
was nowhere concealed in the

landscape. Sweet Lord, I have
come home.

Exile

in the heart of the neighborhood
my dear there is a very big park
you can visit and hold close like
a forest believing it just for your
life in exile. I know you heard
these woodlands will not grow
Mango, Papaya or Cashew trees
but you will eventually learn to
walk, play and rest on its foreign
ground. child some day you will
realize the butchery we fled with
God hidden in it, the mourning
that took place at the church where
soldiers arrested the cross, the mouths
full of words that nightly shouted at
the sky and how death used up the
village peasants and priests. sweet
dear, life began for us here like a
good dream though I know you still
think the Sun in this country will one
day go down never to rise above your
head again. Child, let's give it more
time, light the daily candles, search
for the Angels that fold up the sadness
flight made and try to call this strange
new land home. for now, take my hand
like prayer and call this life your own.

IRON PEN

"O that my words were written down!
O that they were inscribed in a book!
O that with an iron pen and with lead
they were engraved on a rock forever!"
—*Job 19:23–24*

Outcast and utterly alone, Job pours out his anguish to his Maker. From the depths of his pain, he reveals a trust in God's goodness that is stronger than his despair, giving humanity some of the most beautiful and poetic verses of all time. Paraclete's Iron Pen imprint is inspired by this spirit of unvarnished honesty and tenacious hope.

OTHER IRON PEN BOOKS

ABOUT PARACLETE PRESS

PARACLETE PRESS is the publishing arm
of the Cape Cod Benedictine community,
the Community of Jesus. Presenting a full
expression of Christian belief and practice,
we reflect the ecumenical charism of the
Community and its dedication to sacred
music, the fine arts, and the written word.

SCAN
TO
READ
MORE

Learn more about us at our website:

www.paracletepress.com

or phone us toll-free at 1.800.451.5006

YOU MAY ALSO BE INTERESTED IN THESE...

To Shatter Glass
Poems

Sister Sharon Hunter, CJ

ISBN 978-1-64060-714-9 | Hardcover | $24

"In words of courage, conviction, and terrible beauty, Sister Sharon Hunter dispels the myth of escaping life in the real world for the shelter of the cloister. She confronts the lingering demons of the past—a legacy of family alcoholism, abuse, violence, and depression—holding them up to the light of her daily encounters with the mysterious, often incomprehensible, love of God. By reading these poems, we are privileged to join her on the path to hope and healing."

—Sister Helen Prejean,
author of *Dead Man Walking* and *River of Fire: My Spiritual Journey*

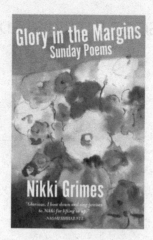

Glory in the Margins
Sunday Poems

Nikki Grimes

ISBN 978-1-64060-677-7 | Hardcover | $22

"Leave it to the sensationally gifted Nikki Grimes to weld her devotions into one glorious body of text. It's possible to feel these deeply rooted poems finding friends even as you read them. They will be spoken in resonant spaces to grateful congregations. They will find new homes in the middle of lonely nights. Generous renderings of familiar biblical stories and precious principles in her own inimitable voice. I bow down to 'An Uncluttered Gospel' and 'Navigating No' among so many gems and sing praises to Nikki for lifting us up."

—Naomi Shihab Nye,
Young People's Poet Laureate, Poetry Foundation

Available at bookstores
Paraclete Press | 1-800-451-5006 | www.paracletepress.com